La Mezzanotte di Spoleto
Midnight in Spoleto

Paolo Valesio

Translation by Todd Portnowitz

Fomite
Burlington, Vermont

Copyright © 2017 Paolo Valesio
Translations copyright © 2017 Todd Portnowitz
Cover image © Lamberto Gentili

All rights reserved. No part of this book may be reproduced in any form or by any means without the prior written consent of the publisher, except in the case of brief quotations used in reviews and certain other noncommercial uses permitted by copyright law.

ISBN-978-1-942515-82-1
Library of Congress Control Number: 2017947981

Fomite
58 Peru Street
Burlington, VT 05401
www.fomitepress.com

Prologo
Fra le quinte del teatro					10

Monteluco
Ecate						22
Monteluco					24
Whistling in the Dark				26
Goodbye, Monteluco . . .			28
Hello, New Haven				30
Confinestate					34
La tentazione della danza			38

Mezzodì e mezzanotte di Spoleto
Mezzodì

Concerto di mezzogiorno			44
Paradiso					46

Mezzanotte
Spettatore notturno				52
Salve, caput cruentatum			54
Paganìa						56
Fonìa						58
Uomo in piedi in un palco di terz'ordine	62
Caligaverunt oculi mei			64

Translator's Note   1
Author's Note   5

Prologue
Among Curtains   11

Monteluco
Hecate   23
Monteluco   25
Whistling in the Dark   27
Goodbye, Monteluco . . .   29
Hello, New Haven   31
Summer's End's Onset   35
The Temptation of Dance   39

Midday and Midnight in Spoleto
Midday

Noon Concert   45
Paradiso   47

Midnight
Nocturnal Spectator   53
Salve, caput cruentatum   55
Paganry   57
Phonic   59
Man Standing in a Third-Tier Box   63
Caligaverunt oculi mei   65

Via Vaita de Domo

Il canone antico	70
Gli animanti (Glossa a san Francesco)	72
Bestiario	76
Frastuonante	80
Il rude calice	82
Attonitamente	84
Desiderii	86
Il mendicante orientale	88
Lo studiante dalle scarpe rotte	90
Ballata gattesca	92
Epitafio verde	96

Sentieri di Francesco

La piscina di annegamento	102
Crociata	104
Natività Novantasette	106
Desiderando parola	108
Preghiera tentatrice	110
Parla una cantatrice in un coro di chiesa	112
La cantatrice all'ascoltatrice	114
Meditazione della rosa	116
Erto nel *despertar*	118
Prossimandosi alla fiamma	120
La sfida	122

Epilogo

San Francesco d'Assisi davanti al bar "Tric-Trac"	126

Via Vaita de Domo

The Ancient Canon	71
The Animated (after St. Francis)	73
Bestiary	77
Deafening	81
Earthen Chalice	83
Dumbfoundedly	85
Desires	87
Beggar from the East	89
The Student with Splitting Shoes	91
A Cat Ballad	93
Green Epitaph	97

Franciscan Trails

The Drowning Pool	103
Cross Mark	105
Nativity Scene Ninety-Seven	107
In Want of Words	109
Tempting Prayer	111
A Female Singer in a Church Choir Speaks	113
The Singer to the Female Listener	115
Meditation on Roses	117
Tall in *Despertar*	119
Drawing Near the Flame	121
The Challenge	123

Epilogue

St. Francis of Assisi Outside of the Cafe "Tric Trac"	127

Notes	133

Translator's Note

Though many people know Paolo Valesio for his work as a scholar—after about three decades of teaching Italian literature in America, principally at Yale and Columbia University—I met him first as a poet. He'd come in 2009 to give a reading at the University of Wisconsin-Madison, where I was a first-year graduate student, deeply afraid that writing papers and writing poems were mutually exclusive activities. Eventually this fear got the best of me and I fled to our country's great orphanage, New York City, where I ran into Paolo again, nearly five years later—and it was on this occasion, in some sense, that the translation of *Midnight in Spoleto* began.

The occasion was a reading by the Italian poet Milo De Angelis, at New York University's Casa Italiana, held to celebrate the publication of *Theme of Farewell and After-Poems* (University of Chicago Press, 2013). The book's pair of English translators, Susan Stewart and Patrizio Ceccagnoli, were there to read alongside De Angelis, and to introduce him was Paolo Valesio, then on the verge of becoming a Professor Emeritus. I couldn't give you a detailed account of his lecture that evening, but I do remember that it centered around the importance of the *citofono* (the door bell phone) in De Angelis's work—a profound metaphor for the labor of the poet, who speaks into one end and whose voice comes out bodiless through the intercom on the other, hoping to reach another soul. (Now I'm wondering how the translator might figure into this—I guess we receive the message and try to relay it through yet another intercom, on an even higher floor? Dare we buzz the poet in?). After the reading I went to shake his hand—who was this man who'd founded two poetry reviews, written two novels, and published numerous works of verse all while remaining a scholar of the highest merit? Soon enough we were talking poetry, then sharing it, then collaborating, over the next three years, on what would become this book.

"Spoleto—the name alone enchants" is the first line of the book's first poem, and if it's true for a native Italian then it's doubly true for an English speaker. Even for this English speaker—though I'd spent a year-and-a-half in Italy and not so far from Spoleto, I'd never heard of the city. I had no sense of its location (middle of the peninsula, in Umbria, south of Perugia), its history (long, of course, and Latin) or of its present reputation (as a city of churches and a city of theater; the city itself a theater, every nook "a barren stage / still fresh with the flitting ghosts / of actors."). It's this last aspect, the mixed presence of religious and secular arenas, that makes it an ideal setting for Valesio's poetry: a walking exegesis, of sorts. Though sustained by concrete description and narrative and set in a very real city, the poems in *Midnight in Spoleto* seem nonetheless to take place in the mind. At every encounter, before every scene or object, the poet cocks his head and considers its symbolic resonance, reading the modern world not only through Christian texts but through the vast body of literature of the last eight centuries and through his own personal history. The actors here are as varied as St. Francis and Francesco Guicciardini, Diderot and Dante, a grasshopper and a monk, the Virgin Mary and Marinetti, all held comfortably within the city's proscenium.

In his brief introduction to the Italian edition, published in 2013 by Raffaelli Editore, Alberto Bertoni describes the poetry that results from so tireless and versatile a mind. Valesio is, he writes,

> a poet who, with the wording and pacing of natural speech, gives expression to a profound polyphony, all centered around a vertiginous play of anachronisms, neologisms ("crucifixional," "Christianizing") or peculiarities of ancient Tuscan prose—oftentimes dotted with or interrupted by keen asides that embrace the experimental.

At such subtlety and rich association, of course, the heart of the reader leaps—the translator's sinks. How will the exactitude be preserved? No equivalent exists! Which meanings will be sacrificed in the exchange? To transport a word's dual meaning safely from one language to another is to walk a cup of hot tea across a tightrope. (But then, occasionally, the tea stays in the cup, and these occasions are the poetry translator's *raison d'être*.)

I've changed nothing about the structure or order of the book, and left any Latin epigraphs in Latin. The notes at the end are the author's, not mine, and they are a revised version of the original Italian text. Though Valesio's syntax, as Bertoni notes, "sounds *other* to the Italian ear," nonetheless "it sacrifices nothing of its fluidity and perspicuity." Particularly with his sonnets,—there are eight of them here—where form and rhyme lead the translator almost inevitably to a stiltedness, I've tried to preserve this fluidity, these artfully altered rhythms of natural speech, by occasionally opting for a trimeter or tetrameter rather than a pentameter. Nearly all of the translations have benefited from Paolo's explanations and edits, and I thank him for the challenge and the pleasure of relaying his words through the English intercom.

Todd Pornowitz
New York, November 2016

Author's Note

The poems in *Midnight in Spoleto* came to being in that city, toward the close of the last century, over the course of a few summers. They revolve around a summer event in Spoleto, the "Festival dei Due Mondi" ("Festival of Two Worlds"): the theater and the church, a sacred place (the church, or the theater?) and a profane place (the theater, or the church?), which also serve as the setting for this narrative. The specific event to which the book owes its title is a series of choral group performances at the ancient church of Sant'Eufemia. Though another constant presence is the surrounding countryside—and between city and country floats the local genie: Saint Francis.

I used the word "narrative" above—and yes, the backdrop to this book is the story of a man and a woman. All self-respecting stories have a beginning, a middle, and an end (which threatens to render the whole production artificial). This story, however, has no respect for itself (that is, it is faithful to life and its winding course). The phase of the story recounted here is the middle—with nothing to say of its beginning or its end, if indeed it has one.

Paolo Valesio
New York, November 2016

Per una ladra di fiori

For a woman who stole flowers

Prologo

"Io vivo nelle ombre dell'ignoranza come un assente"
(Girolamo Savonarola)

Prologue

"I live in the shadows of ignorance like an absentee"
(Girolamo Savonarola)

Fra le quinte del teatro

Spoleto: il mero nome è una magia.
A Spoleto non passeggiavano,
ma si trasferivano: da una strana
occasione in un'altra.
Ogni angolo un deserto palcoscenico
da cui erano appena via guizzati
i fantasmi degli attori
(fantasmi di fantasmi)
lasciando sulle pietre, sulle tavole
sparse qua e là le noci del mistero
i cui gusci lui non poteva frangere;
e trattiene quei frutti sulla palma,
li scruta impenetrabili.
Queste che nelle pagine verranno
sono le scene di Spoleto
su cui ancora medita, che ancora
non ha afferrato.
Lei gli dice:
"Ma insomma questi incontri li hai vissuti,
li hai amati; e allora che aspetti
a passare oltre e vivere il restante?".
Le risponde: "Li ho amati, li ho vissuti
ma non ne sono ancora penetrato.
A Spoleto Francesco si ammalò
e si impennò, riprese
il cammino di Assisi;
e fu il ritorno

Among Curtains

Spoleto—the name alone enchants.
In Spoleto, they didn't stroll,
they ushered themselves
from one strange occasion to another.
Every nook a barren stage,
still fresh with the flitting ghosts
of actors (ghosts of ghosts)
who, in their fleeing, left behind—
on the stones, on the planks scattered
through the city—the kernels of a mystery
whose shells he could not crack;
the fruit totters in his palm,
in his gaze, impenetrable.
What follows in these pages
are scenes from Spoleto
still fixed in his mind,
still far from his grasp.
She says to him:
"So, you've lived these experiences,
you've cherished them, now what do you expect,
to leave it all behind and make a life of what's left?"
"I've cherished them," he replies, "I've lived them,
but I haven't understood them fully.
Spoleto was where Francis grew ill,
where he rose up and resumed
his walk to Assisi—
in Spoleto, he returned

verso la vocazione.
Io, seguitore indegno di colui
(la mia solitudine
non è santitudine),
penso però con mie deboli forze
anch'io al ritorno—ma dove?".

***

Ricorda un pomeriggio in cui la pioggia
affrettava la sera; entrarono
nella chiesa di San Giovanni e Paolo,
non più consacrata al suo uso;
timido e antico (milleesettantaquattro) padiglione
ch'è protetto dalla disattenzione.
Compitarono, con il rispetto
del balbettìo, quattro versi
latini pittati in un cartiglio
accanto al vuoto d'altare:

> "Vox que dixit *Ave*,
> divini nuncia partus,
> *Eve* mutavit nomen,
> opemque tulit".

Discesero poi cauti una scaletta
di legno lungo il muro di sinistra
coi resti di un affresco – picchiettato
(come gli altri in quella
conchiglia di chiesa)
da tante piccole chiazze

to his calling.
And I, his unworthy follower
(my solitude
is not sanctitude)
I, too, have my frail mind
set on a return – but to where?"

          ***

He recalls an afternoon, the rain quickening
evening's arrival. They entered
the church of Saint John and Paul,
unholy in disuse—a feeble and ancient
pavilion (year 1074)
guarded by disregard.
Respectfully, they stammered
through four lines of Latin
inscribed on a scroll
beside the absence of an altar:

> "Vox que dixit *Ave*,
> divini nuncia partus,
> *Eve* mutavit nomen,
> opemque tulit."

They crept down a wooden staircase
along the eastern wall, which bore
a fading fresco—riddled
(as were all the frescoes
in that conch of a church)
with leprous white macules—

di lebbra bianca –
in cui si mostra
il santo vescovo Tommaso Becket
e la sua morte.
Le sue mani risaltano guantate inanellate
sottili mani gotiche estenuate
con dita affusolate
ed elegantemente ripiegate:
la destra blocca la benedizione
in un gesto computatorio
e la sinistra regge
in tenue dandy-equilibrio,
come stelo di un calice o gambo
di un fiore, la pastorale verga.
I suoi assassini sono avvolti
da capo a piedi in corazze
(anche i visi, barrati;
solo emergono occhi di gatto)
e quello più avanzato
leva la spada larga
ma più che a testa o a petto
la lama s'accosta alle mani;
e sembra che, insidiosa e invidiosa,
stia mirando a recidergli le dita.
Escono nella pioggia lasciandosi alle spalle
il murmure delle parole antiche:

depicting the holy bishop Thomas Becket
at the moment of his death.
His hands grace the foreground,
gloved, bejeweled,
slender, gothic hands
with tapered fingers,
elegantly curled:
the right, fixed in a gesture,
like counting items
bestows a benediction,
while the left upholds a crosier,
pinching it daintily
like the stem of a chalice or flower.
His murderers approach,
head-to-toe in plated armor
(even their faces, visored,
showing only slits of eyes).
The nearest hoists his sword.
Though rather than set his mark
on the saint's head or chest—
the blade falls toward his hands,
insidious, envious, as if set
on subtracting his pretty fingers.
They step back into the rain,
abandoning the murmur of ancient words:

"Voce che disse *Ave*,
la nunziatrice del divino parto,
mutò il nome a *Eva*,
a Eva portò aiuto".

***

O Spoleto Spoleto: gli ricorda
che come ebbro vive,
dentro una nube;
che forse non si è ancora risvegliato
dalle mute esistenze precedenti.
Nato secondo anagrafe in Italia –
e a quella radice, fedele –
lui sa però di essere
Renatus a New York.
Si sente a casa soltanto
quando cammina impolverato e solo
lungo certi isolati di Manhattan
o quando sosta, celato
nella folla di certi vestiboli:
Stazione Gran Centrale,
Museo Metropolitano,
Centro Lincoln . . .
Ma ancora prima forse era nato a Spoleto
in una piccola
immemoriale casa
dietro i muri grigio-ocra
nei vicoli sopra e accanto
la cripta di sant'Isacco.

"The voice that uttered *Ave*,
herald of the divine birth,
transformed her name to *Eve*—
and to Eve brougt help."

***

O Spoleto Spoleto: reminder
of how he steps inebriated
through his life in a cloud,
that perhaps he's yet to wake
from the mute momentum of prior selves.
Born in Italy, as the records attest,
and true to his native soil,
he knows himself nevertheless
a Renatus in New York,
at home only when walking,
unkempt and alone,
certain blocks of Manhattan,
or lingering in the crush
of certain vestibules:
Grand Central Station,
The Metropolitan Museum,
Lincoln Center . . .
But perhaps, before any of that,
he was born in Spoleto,
in a small
timeless house
behind the ochre-gray city walls,
set back in one of the alleys

Spoleto città dei teatri:
fra le quinte si aggira. Alza il velame.

above Saint Isaac's crypt.
Spoleto, city of theaters: his days
unfurl among curtains. He draws them back.

Monteluco

"Tutte le strade erranti e tutte le pareti di innocenza si piegano ad incanestrare il Vigneto Umbro"
(F. T. Marinetti)

Monteluco

"Every winding road and every wall of innocence bend like a basket around the Umbrian Vineyard"
                            (F. T. Marinetti)

Ecate

Ogni suo apparire lo stupisce.

L'ha veduta, in questi giorni, crescere
con un'ammirazione
che preparava l'amore
ma che era nutrita di timore.
Ogni sera lasciava che l'umido biancore
invadesse la stanza un poco più.
Ma al momento del sonno
chiudeva gli scuretti.

Ieri notte: nel caldo che scendeva
dal soffitto basso di legno
ricurvo come un ventre di balena,
ha spalancato
la finestrella più vicina al letto.
Si è poi riscosso fra lo scuro e l'alba
prima che si sentissero gli uccelli,
con il petto schiacciato e gli occhi torbi.
Gli era balzata addosso
e il suo bianco malato
aveva offuscato –
gran cappuccio di cobra dispiegato –
il cielo del soffitto.

E stanotte non resta che il cielo
vuoto e rossastro.

Hecate

Her every appearance unnerves him.

He saw her, of late, growing
with an admiration
bordering on love
though fed on fear.
Each evening he let the damp *blancheur*
sink deeper into the walls—
until, on the verge of sleep,
he'd slam the shutters.

Last night: the heat descending
from the low wood ceiling,
arched like the ribs of a whale,
he pushed open
the window nearest his bed.
Again he jolted awake between dark and dawn,
before the birds began, with clouded eyes
and a pressure on his chest.
She'd leaped atop him,
her sickly white
cutting off his vision—
great cobra hood unfolded—
from the sky of the ceiling.

And tonight there's only sky,
rust-red and empty.

Monteluco

"Cum essem in peccatis…"
          (Francesco d'Assisi)

Il bivio è nella pelle e nella mente.

Il presente è essenziale e incomprensibile;
il futuro, inguardabile; il passato
intoccabile.

E resta l'altro: il bivio
del lavoro mentale
(con il cervello teso
a sollevare sacchi
a travasare secchi).
Che cosa fa la mente
con gli anni del peccato?
Può lasciarli cadere –
senza nemmeno bollarli "anni sciupati",
schiacciandoli al disotto del giudizio –
nel vuoto del tempo universo;
o ricercarne con passione il senso:
ogni ora di vita ha da servire –
anche la più sassosa
anche la più fangosa –
a lastricare il cammino
per l'Ascesa del Monte.

Monteluco

"Cum essem in peccatis…"
        (St. Francis of Assisi)

The path splits in the skin and in the mind.

The present is essential and incomprehensible;
the future, unseeable; the past
untouchable.

What remains: the split path
of mental labor
(the brain, braced
for heaving sackfuls,
for tilting bucketfuls).
What's a mind to do
with the years of sin?
Set them adrift—
not even bother to label them "squandered,"
squash them short of judgment—
in the void of cosmic time?
Or go hotly seeking their sense?
Each hour in life must serve—
even the stoniest
even the muddiest—
must pave the way
to the Ascent of the Mountain.

Whistling in the Dark

Che cos'è mai un uomo spirituale?

Cosa precaria e fragile, aperta a tutti i venti.
Sempre attento –
dentro e fuori dall'ombra –
e solo. Perché, attento?
Al buio, il solitario ridiviene bambino:
incoraggia se stesso
e fischia (o prega, o sorride)
rivolto al muro del mondo.

Ma a volte, chi gli arrivi un po' vicino,
lo potrebbe sentire mentre mormora:
"Santa Maria del Cammino".
Fra una parola e l'altra
di questa invocazione
si stendono mille passi e mille e mille.
"Santa – Maria – del – Cammino":
ipnotico dolce declino.
O forse, ascesa.
Ciò che importa è restare fedeli
all'anima del passo
che chiama un altro passo
e così via e sia.

Whistling in the Dark

What creature is he, a spiritual man?

Fragile, precarious thing, exposed to all winds.
Attentive, always—
in and out of shadow—
and alone. But why attentive?
In the dark, the solitary man is a child again,
drawing his own courage
and whistling (or praying, or smiling),
his face to the wall of the world.

But then there were those who inched closer,
who could hear him murmuring:
"Our Lady of the Wayside."
But with a thousand paces, and a thousand,
and a thousand stretched between
each word of the invocation.
"Our – Lady – of – the – Wayside":
hypnotic sweet decline.
Or ascent, perhaps.
What matters is one's faith
in the soul of one's front foot
which calls upon the back—
and so it goes, and is.

Goodbye, Monteluco...

Il corno di corriera è ancora allegro
quando passa la curva non visibile
di là dal viale e il prato e la striscia di bosco;
il fischiare del treno
è ancora melancolico.
Tutto in ordine, dunque – il paesaggio
si adatta alla sua propria descrizione,
si traveste da *locus amoenus*.
Ma il sibilo del vento è già cambiato:
è divenuto oscuro.

Adesso solamente,
sotto il segno di questo avvertimento,
egli quando distende
sopra gli occhi il ricamo delle palpebre
la vede:
abietto obietto della sua peggiore
esausta nostalgia,
la morbida la dolce
più di ogni segno, la rada
l'insenatura oltre il fiume
l'accennante, insensibil
mente declinante – la riva buia.

Mezzo luglio: e l'estate è già finita.

Goodbye, Monteluco . . .

It's still cheerful, the bus's horn,
as they round the hidden curve
past avenue, meadow, strip of forest;
the train's whistle,
still melancholic.
All's in order, then—the countryside
adapts to its description,
outfits itself as *locus amoenus*.
The wind's hiss, though, is changed already,
is already bleak.

Only now,
arrested by this sign,
extending the eyelids'
embroidery over his eyes,
does he see it:
abject object of the lowest,
exhausted nostalgia,
soft, sweet
beyond all signature, the harbor,
the cove past the river,
the nodding, insens-
ibly declining—the dark shore.

Mid-July, and already summer's done with.

Hello, New Haven

Transito
fra l'una e l'altra estate (la seconda
è finita ancora prima dell'inizio).
Ascolta il proprio sangue coagularsi –
nelle canalette
contornanti la rocca del cervello –
con vischiosa lentezza:
è come se una mano
larga forte e asciutta gli premesse,
con graduale sapienza, la carotide.

Ma nessun tocco vi è stato:
che sarebbe poi l'usurato
equivoco gesto,
troppo concreto troppo persistente,
dell'amore;
amore, sì, anche se fosse il colpo
della grazia finale,
il taglio terminatore.

Questo suo roteamento di vertigine
che piano piano gonfia le pupille
di un sangue denso
e sonnolento
è soltanto l'effetto del calore . . .
no, menzogna:
è accaduto perché si è reso conto
(torbido sorride,

Hello, New Haven

Transit
between one summer and another (the latter,
done with before it began).
He listens to the sound of his own blood coagulating –
in the brooks
that run around the rock of his brain –
with a viscous ease:
as if a broad, dry hand were pressing,
with increasing skill,
into his carotid.

But no such contact was made:
though it would have been nothing more
than the hackneyed,
equivocal gesture—
all too dogged and actual —
of love:
love, yes, even if it strike
a final blow,
a culminating grace.

It was the heat that brought it on,
that's all, this spell of vertigo –
his pupils slowly swelling
with a thick and drowsy blood . . .
but no, that wasn't it:
it was the realization

a se stesso rivolto, inorridente)
di essere tornato nel deserto;
e la sua mano, stanca, adesso stenta
a trarre il miele fuori dalle pietre.

(troubled, he smiles
to himself in horror)
that he'd strayed back into the desert;
and his hand now, heavy, strains
to extract honey from the stones.

Confinestate

Oggi vibra per prima volta un segno
di fin'estate:
appena cala il buio s'alza il vento.
Che urla virulento
stravolge i rami, come uomo o donna
di mente intorbidita
nel cuore di una conversazione
lacera delicate ragnatele
di amichevoli scambi
con una voce adirosa.
Ma l'aria è ancora tepida e il contrasto –
tra l'irruzione abrupta e la dolcezza
nel sottocielo –
è sinistro. La stanza
terrena è rabbuiata.
Ha spostato la piccola poltrona
nel centro, a fronte
della portafinestra.
Appena si è seduto e già si alza –
no, si alza solo la sua ombra
fumiginosa incoativa
intenzione cancellata
di abbassare la levetta
che aprirebbe la luce
del riflettore esterno –
esitante ricade seduto
è come se paura l'abbia colto

Summer's End's Onset

Today, the first tremor
of summer's end:
dark falls and at once a wind rises,
virulent, howling,
dispensing with branches,
as a man or a woman
with a troubled mind, disassembles
all the delicate webs
of meaning well
with a single outburst.
But the air is still warm, and the contrast
between the sudden surge and the easy skies
at the horizon,
a touch unsettling. A clouded dark
crowds the ground floor windows.
He's pushed the small chair
to the center of the room,
across from the French doors.
He sits, at last, and at once he stands.
No, only his shadow stands,
smoke-shrouded inchoative,
retracted intention
to flick the switch
that drives the current
to the outdoor floodlights—
hesitant, he sits back down
as if taken by the fear

che l'improvvisa luminosità
improvvida riveli
un mostro reclino
umido di fango
ritratto incomportabile.
Nessuna luce ancora frange il buio.
Egli siede, celato a se stesso.

that the rush of heedless
brightness would reveal
a monster sprawled on the floor,
damp with mud—
impermissible portrayal.
Still, no light disrupts the dark.
He sits, cut off from himself.

La tentazione della danza

Se la pensa la teme; se la sente
con gli scalpiti e i colpi del cuore minacciato
da lei – è come un vento
di desiderio forte e profumato.

Se la teme è vile, e se la brama
è un codardo, affermano i campioni
della vita; i sempre-pronti all'amo
aureo di pervicaci illusioni.

Il terrore ci fa correre innanzi
(dicono) incontro al nemico e al fatale.
È per ciò che lui balza e pare che danzi
un barcollante ballo rozzo e crudo
con la scura fanciulla in-ospitale,
per questo che offre il petto senza scudo?

The Temptation of Dance

To think it is to fear it; to feel it, then,
in the beating of your feet, in the impatient
knock of your threatened heart, is like a wind
of desire—strong and fragrant.

To fear it, only cowardice, to look
too longingly a failure—so conclude
life's vanquishers, those quick to take the hook
and golden bait of obstinate illusions.

Terror (as they'd have it) makes us run
after and into the enemy, to our end.
Could that explain his awkward little jumping
that looks like dancing
with the dark, unyielding girl who beckons him—
why he offers her his chest without a shield?

Mezzodì e mezzanotte di Spoleto

Midday and Midnight in Spoleto

Mezzodì

Midday

Concerto di mezzogiorno

Il gravicembalo
      (l'interno del coperchio è d'albicocca,
      e fiancate di pallido verde
      oliva, nello stile dell'impero)
viaggia indietro su piccole ruote
invisibili e bene temperate
ripercorre in ritroso parallelo
lo sfondo del telone:
un bosco che presto trascende
la nicchia e la statua
per divenire foresta
con scena di fulmine.

      Questo interno viaggio – nella sala
che con gli ori i velluti gli affreschi
si ribella contro il sole
che invisibile da ogni parte assedia –
li ha presi di vertigine.
Escono sulla discensiva
piazza del Duomo
battendo palpebre di pipistrello.

      Teatro Caio Melisso, Spoleto

Noon Concert

The harpsichord
        (its lid with an apricot underside
        lined with pale olive
        green, in the Empire style)
retreats on little wheels,
well-tempered and invisible,
reversing on a parallel
through the curtain backdrop:
a wood that fast transcends
niche and statue
to become forest
with a lightning scene.

        This internal voyage – in a room
that with its golds, velvets, and frescoes
rebels against the invisible
siege of the circling sun –
struck them with vertigo.
They exit down the sloping
cathedral square,
flicking their flittermouse eyelids.

        The Caio Melisso Theater, Spoleto

Paradiso

> "L'acteur est las, et vous triste; c'est qu'il s'est démené sans rien sentir, et que vous avez senti sans vous démener"
> (Denis Diderot, *Paradoxe sur le comédien*)

Il paradiso piccolo con l'arco
del soffitto affrescato
che quasi tocca la testa:
il loggione del Caio Melisso.
Ecco: il gran lampadario
al centro del soffitto – di poche braccia
distante – si spegne
ma le piccole luci dei palchi
restano accese qualche instante ancora.
Poi, il buio; ma presto si rivela
la luce, doppiamente artificiale,
della scena denudata, al segnale
degli orchestrali in basso.
L'opera che si srotola in questa matinée
è un inferno dolce e bonario;
inferno di salotto e *boudoir* –
color di pesca
lievemente inturgidita
pieno di specchi e gabbie e pappagalli
e divani turcheschi.
E non importa quale poi sia il dramma
in questa mattinata;
chi s'agita su quelle assi è Dives,
e chi osserva dalla piccionaia

Paradiso

> "The actor is spent, you're unhappy; he's exerted himself
> without feeling, you've felt without exertion"
> (Denis Diderot, *The Paradox of Acting*)

Little heaven with an arch
of its frescoed ceiling
grazing their heads:
the *loggione* at Caio Melisso.
Here they are: the grand chandelier
at the ceiling's center—a few arm lengths
above—goes out,
but the little stage lights
burn another instant.
Then, darkness. But soon, a sign
from the orchestra pit
and a light appears, doubly artificial,
on an empty stage.
The opera this matinée
is a sweet hell of good intentions;
a hell of salon and boudoir—
peach-colored,
somewhat swollen,
full of mirrors, cages, parrots,
Turkish sofas.
And whatever's plotted here today
is of no import;
that man exerting himself on stage, there, is Dives,
and up in the peanut gallery, looking on,

è un Lazzaro: egli spera
che un volo di colombe lo porti in paradiso,
al benvenuto di Abramo.

some Lazarus, hoping
a flock of doves will carry him to heaven
and into the lap of Abraham.

Mezzanotte

Midnight

Spettatore notturno

Silenziosamente invoca:
   'Tienimi
le palpebre sollevate
quella specialmente
che troppo greve cala
sull'occhio sinistro.
Temo le tenebre
ancora più di quanto io paventi
la luce'.

                Primo coro della mezzanotte
              ("San Francisco Girls Chorus")
                  Chiesa di S. Eufemia

Nocturnal Spectator

Silently he pleads:
  'Hold
open my eyelids,
especially the one
falling so finally
over my left eye.
I fear the shadows
even more than I dread
the light.'

                First midnight choir
                ("San Francisco Girls Chorus")
                      Church of St. Euphemia

Salve, caput cruentatum

> "Or questa, or quella corda"
> (Girolamo Savonarola)

Lei, *capa 'e muorta*, cranio d'Irochese
sotto cresta di rigidi capelli
ombra punk ma composta come marmo
schiava cristiana in casta scollatura –
le corde del suo smagro collo,
che emerge da un busto
statuario ma esusto,
si tendono per lauda:
fili di marionette
nel teatro crocefissionale.

> Secondo coro della mezzanotte
> ("I Laudesi Umbri")

Salve, caput cruentatum

> "Now this chord, now that one"
> (Girolamo Savonarola)

She, like the skull or scalp of an Iroquois
under a crest of hardened hair,
punk-rock with a marble composure,
Christian slave with a chaste neckline—
the cords of her gaunt neck
rising from a scorched
though statuary bust,
stretch in praise:
puppet strings
in the crucifixional theater.

> Second midnight choir
> ("I Laudesi Umbri")

Paganìa

Oggi dietro le femmine del coro,
dietro le cristiananti americane,
si vede un altro e differente ploro:
i volti di due tragiche estranee.

Una ha la faccia di Elena argiva
sotto il fitto capello ramato;
e la mano che incerta la scolpiva
le ha dato un naso nobile e scorciato.

L'altra ha il viso di adultera assassina
terrea e stanca ed anziana:
devastata da sua propria rapina,

rïafferma l'aridità pagana –
eredità della tribù d'Atreo –
e strappa il cuore alla parola "reo".

                Terzo coro della mezzanotte
              ("Coro del Festival di Spoleto")

Paganry

Today, behind the choir girls, behind
the bevy of Christianizing statesiders
one sees a mournfulness of a different kind:
the faces of two tragic outsiders.

The first has the face of Argive Helen, capped
by a copper set of hair; and, as it goes,
the less than steady hand that gave her shape
left her with a noble half-a-nose.

The other has the face of a two-timing
murderer, pale and tired and elderly:
robbed of all by a crime of her own doing.

She reaffirms her pagan nudity—
an inheritance from the tribe of Atreus—
and tears the heart from the word "ignominious."

> Third midnight choir
> ("Spoleto Festival Choir")

Fonìa

> "Come la cerva anela ai corsi d'acqua
> così l'anima mia a te, Signore"
> (Salmo 42)

Fiamma lambente,
lingua plangente.

Torna il daino alla fonte:
per la seconda volta il Salmo suona –
la prima era al concerto dei Laudesi,
la terza avverrà fra due giorni –
balzando dalla pagina marcata
di un enorme volume ingabbiato
in cuoio corrugato,
con una sua catena segnalibro,
che aspetta su un leggìo damascato
al centro di un basso salone,
come il pilastro d'un destino.

I volti caro-estranei nella folla
cadono insieme come foglia a foglia:
smorta, o di rimembranze colorita,
o fresca di pioggia scrollata.
Umbri volti affratellati:
i visi forestieri sono cari
(sorelle improbabili, fratelli);
i volti dei propri cari
sono laceranti.

Phonic

> "As the hart panteth after the water brooks
> so panteth my soul after thee, O God"
> Psalm 42 (KJV)

Lambent flame,
plangent tongue.

The fawn returns to its spring:
a second time, the Psalm is sounded—
the first, at the concert of the Flagellants,
the third, to come in two days—
leaping off the tabulated page
of an enormous volume, bound
in corrugated leather,
a chain for a bookmark,
perched on a damask-draped lectern
at the center of a grand basement,
like the pillar of a destiny.

In the crowd, the dear faces of strangers
fall together, leaf on leaf—
pale, or tinged with remembrance,
or fresh, the rain shook from their skin.
A fold of Umbrian faces:
the grins of guests are dear
(improbable sisters, brothers)
while those most dear
injure in appearance.

Ma carità dell'occhio è insufficiente—
è alibi di non spirituale cuore;
questa virtù si misura
con lo scandaglio del fango.

Lingua lambente,
come il cervo nell'acqua del torrente,
fiamma plangente.

Quarto coro della mezzanotte
("Camerata Polifonica Viterbese")

But an eye's empathy is insufficient—
an alibi for a heart detached from spirit;
such virtue can be measured
only by plumbing a pool of mud.

Lambent tongue,
like a deer in a rushing stream,
plangent flame.

                      Fourth midnight choir
              ("The Polyphonic Camerata from Viterbo")

Uomo in piedi in un palco di terz'ordine

> "E non sai tu che nel mistero
> tu mi rapisti ogni pensiero,
> tu m'ispirasti la virtù?"
> (Dall'*Evgenij Onegin* di Čajkovskij)

Qual voce se non la sua,
silenziario del suo silenzio,
risulta udita e non-udita quando
piega la cordanervo dell'arco
di volontà ad essere paziente
di muso e museruola, altrui o suo?

Ripensando, durante l'opera (nel Teatro Nuovo),
al Quinto coro della mezzanotte
("Orchestra e coro del Festival di Spoleto")

Man Standing in a Third-Tier Box

> "Don't you know that, in the mystery,
> you stole my every thought,
> you inspired virtue within me?"
> (From Tchaikovsky's *Eugene Onegin*)

Whose voice, if not his,
the silentiary of his silence,
is heard and unheard when
the mindstring slackens on the bow
of his will, in tolerance
of snout and muzzle, his or another's?

>   An afterthought, during the opera
> (at the Teatro Nuovo) of the Fifth midnight choir
>   ("The Spoleto Festival Orchestra and Choir")

Caligaverunt oculi mei

I peregrini del sacrato canto
come neri si avviano felini:
uomini e donne in fila pazienti sotto il giogo
dell'arte che a se stessi hanno imposto
verso l'abside nell'ora
malata nell'ora
della mortalità perlacea
nell'ora senza notte e senza giorno
quando si vive solo per scommessa
quando tutto è consunto è ripetuto
fino alla stoltezza –
eppure la ripetizione
è la fonte di giustificazione.

E questi pellegrini, onde scavarono
la loro musica?
Sotto mucchi e ruine di cadaveri
dentro i profondi strati
dei teschi e dei frammenti?

Gli sopra viene alla mente
il loro camminare silenzioso
prima di incorollarsi
in semicerchio e cantare,
quando reca il suo tributo
alla consumazione delle pietre:
le squadrate, le nere

Caligaverunt oculi mei

The pilgrims of the sacred responsory
slink cat-like black into song:
a line of men and women, calm beneath the yoke
of an art they've laid upon their own necks,
toward the apse in the hour
ill in the hour
of an opaline mortality,
in the hour without night or day
when life hangs on a bet,
when all is ragged and repeated
into blank stupidity—
and yet the repetition
is the source of justification.

And these pilgrims,
where do they dig up their music?
Beneath the heaps and remains of corpses,
down in the deeper strata
of skulls and bone fragments?

Their silent wayfaring
sails up into his thoughts
before the pilgrims bloom
into a semicircle and sing,
as he pays homage
to the stones' consumption,
the squares, the shades of black

che sembrano unte o bagnate
di qualche fatalità
che giù discenda insieme con la sera.

Il selciato
di Piazza del Mercato
gli è saltato agli occhi
(ha subìto un attacco di vertigine)
come il muso della morte.
Vorrebbe rifugiarsi ai pellegrini,
dietro il loro muro di canto.
Ma questo
è il consiglio della viltà.
Lo deve ricacciare: solo resta
con la sua nudità.

Sesto coro della mezzanotte
("Coro Polifonico di Reggio Emilia")

greased, almost, or slick
with some tragic fate
sliding down, along with evening.

The pavement
of Piazza del Mercato
snapped up at his eyes
(in a vertiginous daze)
like the snout of death.
Why not blend among the pilgrims,
take refuge behind their wall of song?
But that
would be a coward's way out.
He must smother it: only him now
and his nakedness.

Sixth chorus of midnight
("Reggio Emilia Polyphonic Choir")

Via Vaita de Domo

Via Vaita de Domo

Il canone antico

Gli animali sono canonizzati
dalla mite processione
del loro sguardo
forse curioso forse no
quando (nei radi istanti quando)
muove incontro-scontro a noi.
Una volta – milioni di anni scorsi –
vigeva tra essi e gli umani
la sacertà del reciproco terrore.
Adesso la paura
siede in loro soltanto.
Lo sguardo degli umani è laicizzato
quello degli animali è ipnotizzato.
In questi tempi sono accomunati
in rischio differente
da quello dell'artiglio e della clava:
essere colti insieme, raggelati
fino allo sfondo della paralisi,
dal grande obiettivo.
Come con-batterlo?
Cercando (non vi sono garanti)
svicoli e camminamenti
di selvatico amore
che spesso di sé ride.

The Ancient Canon

Animals are canonized
by the easy back-and-forth
of their gazes,
whether curious or not,
when (those rare occasions)
they connect-collide with our own.
Once—millions of years ago —
the sanctitude of reciprocal terror
held court between man and animal.
Now that fear
rests with them alone.
The human gaze is laicized,
the animal gaze hypnotized.
They're united in these times
by a risk far different
than claw or club:
of being gathered together, frozen
through to the core of paralysis,
by the wide camera lens.
How to combat it?
By looking (there are no guarantees)
for the back alleys and byways
of a primal love, given
to laughing at itself.

Gli animanti (Glossa a san Francesco)

Regno animale e regno vegetale
e regno umano e regno angelicale:
i confini sembrano
indebolirsi come in una nebbia –
paiono graffi, superficialmente
graffiti e graffiati
sopra la pelle del mondo.

      Cerchio degli animali,
degli animati animanti –
metamorfico cerchio.
Uno stormo di uccelli sopra un albero:
chiacchiericciano come
(pare che Béla Bartók abbia detto
in una sua lettera)
scimmie.
Gli uccelli come scimmie
le scimmie come uomini
gli uccelli fluttuanti
nell'aria come pesci
gli uccelli sono spiriti
dispersi poi subito ripresi
al volo, spiriti contesi
tra gli angeli e gli umani
gli uccelli sono angeli
rimpiccioliti
ma restano aggraziati

The Animated (After St. Francis)

Animal kingdom and vegetable kingdom
kingdom of humans and kingdom of angels:
the borders seem
to blur as in a fog—
scratches appear, superficially
scratched and scrawled
on the skin of the world.

    Circle of animals,
of animating animals—
metamorphic circle.
A throng of birds above a tree:
chitter-chattering
(as Béla Bartók, it would seem,
wrote in a letter)
like monkeys.
Birds like monkeys
monkeys like men
birds wavering
in the air like fish
birds are spirits
fanning out, regrouping
in flight, spirits contested
by angels and men
birds are angels
in miniature
though graceful still

gli uccelli sono angeli terricoli.

    Gli animali, tutti, sono
agli uomini quasi eguali.
Ma i confini non sono cancellati:
attraverso questi, gli sguardi
si reciprocamente interrogano
con separato rispetto
(non vedono più l'altro come oggetto).
Come gli angeli, gli animali
richiamano in questione
l'affaticata congiunzione
di corpo e d'anima.
È forse per questo che sono
più belli degli uomini –
appesantiti dall'anima
che si portano in petto.

birds are earthbound angels.

        Animals, all animals,
are the near equal of men.
But the boundaries remain:
their questioning gazes
cross the borders
with separate respect
(no longer seeing the other as object).
Like angels, animals
call back into question
the belabored union
of body and soul.
Which perhaps is why
they're more beautiful than men—
weighed down by the *anima*
in their chests.

Bestiario

> "Respecte dans la bête un esprit agissant"
> (Gérard de Nerval)

Amando le creature d'insondabile cuore
si evita lo scambio dell'amore
e si ricerca un facile tesoro
volendo discansarsi
dai propri sentimenti.
È una cosa assai triste, quando il cuore
non trova più parole.
Rimane la speranza della chiocciola
nella sua striscia
lungo-attraverso il muro
illusiva d'immortalità.
Ma che accade alla vita
tra l'ora delle cicale
e quella dei pipistrelli?
È umana vita, o ferina?

I felini lungo il muro
sulla crosta e la cresta della pietra
si studiano e si assottigliano
in qualche vana ricerca:
sperdutezza
di una notte senz'anima.
Vi è più anima invero (e meno vita)
nello scuretto
che batte la disperata

Bestiary

> "Respect an animal's active spirit"
> (Gérard de Nerval)

In training your love on the unfathomable heart
of animals, you dodge reciprocation,
in search of a simpler treasure:
to dispossess yourself
of your own emotions.
It's as sad as it seems, when the heart
can find no words.
What's left is the hope of the snail,
the trail it leaves,
along-across the wall,
of illusory immortality.
But what happens in a life
between the cicadas' hour
and the hour of the bats?
Life—is it human or savage?

The felines along the wall
on the rough ridge of stone
deepen and sharpen their senses
in the name of some vain pursuit:
the placelessness
of a soulless night.
There's more soul, in truth (and less life)
in the shutter
that slams like a desperate alarm

sul muro del palazzo Della Genga
perché ci si può illudere che il vento
sia mano che lo muove.
Cala il cielo al momento del cobalto
e quelli che punteggiano il pendìo
si avvicinano – (ognuno
lungo la sua linea
diversa e agli altri ostile), pazïenti,
vagamente supplici, loschi
(i poveri non possiedono
il lusso dell'innocenza) –
alla bassa inferriata e porta chiusa;
e il gitano più giovane
comincia a miagolare
per sedurre qualcuna
delle americanine dentro il residence:
che fuori esca furtiva
con la scodella degli avanzi
premuta contro il seno.
Sanno una cosa, una cosa
così uguale a se stessa
che a un umano annuvola il cervello
e lo agonizza di monotonia:
sanno che ogni notte
è un appuntamento scivoloso,
pazzamente rischioso,
dispietatamente vischioso.

up in the Della Genga palace—
at least then one can pretend
that wind was the hand that brought it shut.
The sky descends in a flush of cobalt
and the figures dotting the slope
draw nearer one another, each
cutting its own distinct path,
hostile to the others—patient,
mildly supplicant, sly
(the poor do not have
the luxury of innocence).
And by the low grating, the closed door;
the youngest gypsy
begins to meow
in an effort to seduce
the American girls inside:
one girl slips out the door
pressing a bowl of leftovers
to her bosom.
And there's one thing they know,
one thing so identical to itself
that it clouds the human brain
and strains it with monotony:
that each and every night
is a slippery arrangement,
wild with risk,
mercilessly viscid.

Frastuonante

Cani galli campane pigolii
di vari e volanti
rullìo dell'autostrada
dentro la gola della valle.
Quando preme i talloni delle mani
sopra le sfere degli occhi
il circolo fra il suono e il rumore
si arresta e si trasforma
in un buio quadrato di quietudine;
austerità improvvisa che ammonisce
più di qualunque tocco di campana.

Deafening

Dogs roosters bells chirps,
various and aerial,
the highway's drumroll
in the throat of the valley.
When he presses the heels of his hands
to the spheres of his eyes
the flow between sound and noise
stops and transforms
into a darkness framed in calmness—
austerity, no less, a calling forth
clearer than the stroke of any bell.

Il rude calice

In un momento suo di ozio-pensiero
rade col cucchiaino il caffè e zucchero
sul fondo della grande tazza rustica
e in quel gorgo il suo sguardo si smarrisce
e poi si risolleva
solamente per perdersi di nuovo
nel paesaggio oltre la ringhiera.
Avvolge in quel minuscolo
cratere di terraglia
la dolcezza sinistrata
della valle spoletina
e poi con un soppiatto lo ricopre
e lo posa sul banco
di pietra così tiepida
che sembra tenera.
Ma il vento sbalza
e volteggia e scoperchia:
il paese liberato
ritorna all'abbondanza del suo cielo.

Earthen Chalice

During one of his spells of idle thought,
stirring his *caffè*, kicking up sugar
from the bottom of a rustic teacup
his gaze smears in the swirl,
resurfaces,
only to stray again
toward the landscape beyond the balustrade.
In that miniscule
crater of crockery,
the skewed suavity
of Spoleto's valley
turns twice
before he caps it with the saucer
and sets it on a bench
so warm its stone
seems supple.
But the wind leaps, whirls
and overturns the lid:
the land set free,
restored to its plenitude of sky.

Attonitamente

Il rondone, più tardo nel suo volo
e più robusto,
s'imbosca fra i cespugli dentro il brolo.
Le rondini, che sono più leggere –
di quella levità
che non si sa
se sia disperazione oppure gioia –
svolano nel frattanto a metà cielo.
Di contro
alla facciata di San Nicolò,
nell'ombra luminosa
(il sole è ancora troppo alto
sopra la valle),
filano i colombacci
le loro evoluzioni
di argento a stormi
dividenti, declinanti.
A che mai giova il moto,
a che la quiete?

Dumbfoundedly

A swift, slower in flight
and more robust,
buries itself in the backyard hedges.
Swallows, far lighter—
of that levity
one might fairly call
desperation or joy—
meanwhile cruise mid-sky.
Across from the façade
of San Nicolò,
in a luminous shadow
(the sun still too high
above the valley)
wood pigeons parade
their evolutions
of silver in dividing,
descending throngs.
What did motion ever bring,
what did stillness?

Desiderii

Quasi occorre ogni giorno e ricorre:
il desiderio di una mano
che rapida emergendo
dalle lagune della terra
con carità chirurgica trascorra
lungo la gola
tagliando la miseria della vita.

Quasi occorre ogni giorno e ricorre:
il desiderio di una mano
che spinga urga prema fin che passi
il molle muro delle nubi e cielo
e si posi alla fine sulla spalla –
ravvivante tocco; ma sopra tutto
orientamento di dovere
e di interna giustizia: per potere
ritrovare la sorgiva
da cui esce e geme il fiume
della conversazione con il mondo.

Desires

It rises and rises again, almost daily:
the desire for a hand
to spring forth
from the earth's lagoons
and run with a surgical grace
along the throat,
excising misery from life.

It rises and rises again, almost daily:
the desire for a hand
to push, press, urge until it passes
through the soft wall of clouds and sky
and comes to a rest at last on one's shoulder—
reviving touch; but above all
the sure compass of duty
and inner justice: the will
to rediscover the source
that feeds the wauling river
of conversation with the world.

Il mendicante orientale

Quando l'ombra sua si allunga
sopra i mattoni aranci del terrazzo
e i sandali schiaffeggiano la pietra
e la rossa maglietta e pantaloni gialli
si rincrudiscono sotto il sole
che già percuote l'orlo delle otto –
quale ombra di monaco è mai questa,
assolato in vagante solitudine
avvolto vagamente di tinta zafferana
pronto a scendere la scalea
verso le campagne i boschi
la polvere dei sentieri
l'aria che gli rimbalza le sue stesse parole
senza nemmeno il sostegno
di un vento di campane?

Beggar from the East

When his shadow lengthens
on the terrace's orange tiles
and his sandals slap the stone
and his red shirt and yellow pants
blanch in the sun, already
playing at the edges of 8 AM—
what shade of a monk is this,
astray in vagrant solitude,
tinged with an aura of saffron,
easing his way down
the stairs to the fields, the forests,
the dust-matted paths,
the wind, bringing back his own words
and nothing else, not even a lilting
draft of distant bells?

Lo studiante dalle scarpe rotte

Sul terrazzo di cotto le farfàllule
s'aggirano fra le campànule
e lui, flip-flap, cammina avanti e indietro
con rumore sandàlico da spiaggia
ma con mano-leggìo regge i *Ricordi*
che in margini postilla
con – unico suo lusso – la matita
automatica e dorata.

The Student with Splitting Shoes

On the terracotta terrace, butterflies
flutter in and out of trumpet flowers
while, flip-flop, he goes pacing up and down
with a beach-day sandal slap, though propped
in his lectern-hand is a copy of the *Ricordi,*
in the margins of which he scrawls
with his one and only luxury: a pencil—
gold-plated and mechanical.

Ballata gattesca

> "Tybalt, you rat-catcher, will you walk? [...]
> Good King of Cats"
> (W. Shakespeare, *Romeo and Juliet,* 3.1)

I.

Tebaldo fa una vita clandestina
da gatto di cantina
vicino al residence –
appare e spare sotto una finestra
donde ogni tanto una studentessina
gli butta giù un brandello di porchetta.
Ma una sera all'ora del Calante
la studenta non getta la carne;
gli legge a voce alta
questa piccola storia post-buddista:

"Nansen vide i monaci dell'ala orientale e quelli dell'ala occidentale che si disputavano un gatto. Afferrò il gatto e disse ai monaci: 'Se qualcuno di voi dice una buona parola, potete salvarlo'. Nessuno rispose, sicché Nansen, intrepido, tagliò in due il gatto. Quella sera tornò Joshu, e Nansen gli raccontò l'accaduto. Joshu si tolse i sandali, se li mise in testa, e andò via. Nansen disse: 'Se ci fossi stato tu, avresti potuto salvare il gatto' ".

A Cat Ballad

> "Tybalt, you rat catcher, will you walk? […]
> Good King of Cats"
> (W. Shakespeare, *Romeo and Juliet*, 3.1)

I.

Tybalt leads the clandestine life
of a wine cellar cat,
just off the main house—
appearing and disappearing below the window
where, now and then, a schoolgirl
throws him a scrap of *porchetta*.
But one evening, at the fall of twilight,
the girl throws no meat;
instead she reads the cat
this little post-Buddhist tale:

Nansen saw the monks of the eastern and western halls fighting over a cat. He seized the cat and told the monks: "If any of you say a good word, you can save the cat." No one answered. So Nansen boldly cut the cat in two pieces. That evening Joshu returned and Nansen told him about this. Joshu removed his sandals and, placing them on his head, walked out. Nansen said: "If you had been there, you could have saved the cat."

II.

I gatti: i fratellini, i fratellastri
i catti sempre intenti
a cattare cosine per terra
lungo via Vaita de Domo –
loro duca è Tebaldo,
comanda a tutti i gatti della strada.
Nessuno degli umani
(poche anime, peraltro)
che meriggiano dietro le persiane
sa chi egli sia; è il guerriero inafferrabile.

Ma all'alba dopo la notte
in cui finisce il Festival, la notte
dei fuochi d'artificio,
lo trovano impiccato dalla grata
della finestra all'angolo sassoso
dove la strada intoppa
contro il muro che dà la scalata
al palazzo Della Genga,
e più sopra,
al cielo e al Duomo.

II.

Cats: little brothers, half-brothers
always intent
on snatching objects from the ground
along Via Vaita de Domo—
Tybalt is their grand duke,
leader of all the street cats.
Not one of the humans
(though there's only a few)
napping behind the curtains
knows who he is: the elusive warrior.

But at dawn, after the last night
of the Festival, the night
with fireworks, they found him
hanging from a window grate
in the rocky corner
where the street dead-ends
into the wall that leads to the stairs
to Palazzo Della Genga,
and still higher,
to the heavens and the Duomo.

Epitafio verde

Sta rileggendo un classico italiano
(così asciutto e toscano
che allega il palato della mente)
in una stanza grande seminuda
alto-soffittata
avaramente illuminata –
e un forte fruscìo
venuto dalla notte irrompe in camera
lo forza a levare lo sguardo
con un tenero senso di nausea
perché, pensa, sarà un pipistrello.
Nulla vede, e riabbassa
lo sguardo appuntito (in lotta
contro la luce annebbiata)
sulle pagine aguzze.
Ma il frùscio si ripete – è ricostretto
a sollevare gli occhi nebulosi
poi li abbassa verso il pavimento:
là si sbatte grossa e saltella
una cavalletta
stupendamente verde.
Ha il fatato colore di smeraldo
del paradiso-inferno amazzonico;
è come una fibula di giada
sul rosso seno dell'ammattonato.
È ipnotizzata o ipnotica?
Resterà il suo segreto.

Green Epitaph

He's rereading an Italian classic
(so dry and Tuscan
it piques the mental palate)
in an oversized and under-furnished room,
high-ceilinged,
stingily lit—
when a loud rustling
from the night breaks in
and he's forced to lift his gaze
with a vague sense of nausea,
certain he'll find a bat.
Nothing there, he lowers
his eyes again (narrowed
in a strain against the dark)
to the stark pages.
But the rustling repeats—again
he lifts his bleary eyes
then turns them quickly to the ground,
where a massive grasshopper lands
and leaps—stupendously green,
the fated emerald
of the Amazonian heaven-hell—
like a jade fibula
cradled by the brick red floor.
Hypnotized or hypnotic?—
its own little secret.
Three times

Per tre volte
catturata (ogni volta
dopo una lotta scivolosa
con l'aiuto di una scodella),
egli la posa sopra il davanzale
aperto sulla notte e sulle mura
arcaiche della sua strada più amata.
Ed essa per tre volte
fugge la libertà e risalta indietro
dentro la stanza mortale.
Si occulta, infine,
dietro la panca di legno.
Dopo un'ora egli stuta la luce,
la lascia in compagnia del proprio scheletro.

he captures it (each time,
after a slippery assault
with a cereal bowl),
and places it on a window sill
open to the night
and the archaic city walls
along his best loved street.
And all three times
it shirks its freedom,
leaps back into the mortal room,
concealing itself in the end
behind a wooden bench.
After an hour he kills the light
and leaves it alone with its own skeleton.

Sentieri di Francesco

"Nil jucundius vidi valle mea spoletana"
(Francesco d'Assisi)

Franciscan Trails

"Nil jucundius vidi valle mea spoletana"
(Francesco d'Assisi)

La piscina di annegamento

Per Dante Alighieri
(*Inferno* XVI, 124-136)

Quando dice: "Signore non son degno . . . "
e poi giunge alla clausola ascendente:
"Ma dì una parola solamente . . . "
gli pare vedere una fune
che cala nel subacqueo silenzio
e tocca la fronte
di lui che stava annegando
senza osarselo dire; l'afferra
e lento tendendo
e alternatamente raggruppando
le gambe come rana o palombaro
sale attraverso strati di acqua e vita
emerge dal fondo
bello e orribile, attinge
la superficie crudamente solare –
la salvazione piatta.

The Drowning Pool

For Dante Alighieri
(*Inferno* XVI, 124-136)

When he says, "Lord, I am not worthy . . . "
and, reaching the ascendant clause,
"but only say the word . . ."
he seems to see a rope
descend through subaqueous silence
and touch the forehead
of the man drowning yet unwilling
to admit it. He seizes it,
and, slowly extending,
alternately gathering
his legs, like a frog or a deep-sea diver,
rises through strata of water and life,
emerges from the awful depths, breaks
the crudely solar surface—
flat salvation.

Crociata

Quella croce fluorescente incisa
su terreo volto di casìpola –
cicatrice a colpo di fulmine
schiaffo livido in faccia alla facciata
che con questa incisura si disvela
possibile luogo ecclesiale
(cospirazione spirituale).
E intanto alla tarda delle otto
il tramonto mantiene un suo orlo
sontuoso sottonube
e minaccia un altro lusso:
quello della tempesta.
Che però si è, pare, accontentata
di aver lanciato quella crocefulmine
sulla casa, che prima del fendente
forse non era chiesa.

Cross Mark

Fluorescent cross incised
in the cottage's earthen visage—
scar of a lightning strike,
livid slap in the face of the façade,
revealed, by this incision,
as potentially ecclesial
(conspiration of the spiritual).
Meanwhile, nearing nine,
the sunset holds its hem,
cloud-covered and sumptuous,
threatening a further luxury: a storm.
Though as it stands, it seems well satisfied,
having hurled that lightning-cross
at the house, which, for all we know,
may not have been a church
before it struck.

Natività Novantasette

Il giorno è rosso come rossa è stata
la notte della Vigilia
alla messa di ninna e di nanna.

Il giorno è rosso, ma nel suo trascorso
la unica politica che vale
è quella della contemplazione.

Il giorno è rosso anche a cielo grigio
perché rosso è il sentiero
che – striscia di foresta,
attraverso le foglie macerate
e gli squarciati porporini fiori
dello scialle velluto (nel colorato
pacchetto lacerato) –
può condurre alla e oltre
soglia dell'anno di muschio
trinato di neve e perlato.

Nativity Scene Ninety-Seven

The day is red, as was the night
of Christmas eve
at the Mass of Mother Goose.

The day is red, but in its passing
the only worthy politics
is contemplation.

Even beneath gray skies, the day is red,
because the path is red
—strip of forest
made with macerated leaves
and the crimson flower shreds
of a velvet shawl (in the bright,
torn package)—
that leads to and beyond
the threshold of this moss-hung year
beaded and laced with snow.

Desiderando parola

Ogni giorno che vola, egli sente
dentro di sé un rombo premente:
son le parole che vorrebbe dire
prima che scocchi l'ora del finire,

le parole accorrenti a tutti quelli
che ha scoperto essere fratelli
e sorelle (se alcune furono amate
più d'altre, invidie e insidie son passate).

S'egli rappresentasse ad ogni uno
l'onda della vita come un dono,
riscatterebbe la sua tramontante

esistenza oscura e pesante
che non trova in se stessa più valore
se non nel tuttassurdo dell'amore.

In Want of Words

With every day that slips, he feels the roar—
growing in him, pressing at his sides—
of all the words he'd like to say before
the arrow of his final hour flies.

Words that speed their way to all the brothers
and sisters he discovered in life (alas,
if for a time he loved some more than others
the jealousy and pettiness have passed).

If he could find a way to give each one
his lifetime as a wave, a sort of gift,
it would reignite the heavy, setting sun

of his darkening existence—all but stripped
of meaning, with the small exception of
that absolute absurdity called love.

Preghiera tentatrice

A ogni alba un impeto oscuro
lo caccia verso la foresta o muro
di alberi-desideri di morire
di sentieri-evasioni dal patire

nel cui fondo un lùmine rosseggia:
guida dentro i budelli della reggia
dell'inferno. Egli prega un carme austero
ma sregolato, e contrariante al vero:

preghiera di un diabolico fabbro
che sconcerta e sconsacra il mattutino
che interrompe mordendosi il labbro

che più tardi lo fa sentir meschino
quando il sole di annunzio immeritato
gli dice: 'Anche oggi ti ha salvato'.

Tempting Prayer

Every dawn, some foreign calling
sends him to the forest, to a wall
of trees like cries for death,
trails that wend around all effort—

a flush of red light at the end—
that lead into the bowels of the den
of hell. He mutters a prayer, harsh
but unruly, opposed to the truth,

a prayer of the devil's making
that disturbs and defiles the morning,
that he clamps behind his teeth,

that later makes him seethe
with shame, when the sun undeservedly maintains:
  "Yes, He saved you, even today."

Parla una cantatrice in un coro di chiesa

Se apro il canoro libro
e a esso volgo lo sguardo,
gli abbandono la gola e la voce
prima della mente
socchiudendo il seno
prima ancora di schiudere il cervello
al senosenso di quello spartito.
Ogni pagina rivoltata
può essere un taglio di ascia
e forse mi giungerà
la sorte di quella santa
in Alessandria:
già stesa sopra i denti della ruota
le vibrarono un colpo di mannaia
(compassione o impazienza?) e dal collo
latte sprizzò non sangue.
Il mio strumentale corpo
è una canna scavata:
versa il latte del canto,
spruzza come un turibolo impazzito
verso di voi nell'ombra
delle rossastre navate.

A Female Singer in a Church Choir Speaks

When I open a hymnbook
and lower my eyes
my throat and voice take off
before my mind,
half-revealing my breast
before even exposing my brain
to the sheet music's soulsense.
Every page-turn
cleaves like an ax.
My fate, perhaps,
is that of the saint
in Alexandria,
stretched over the teeth of a wheel—
down swings the blade
(compassion or impatience?) and milk,
not blood, streams from her neck.
My instrumental body
is a hollow reed,
pouring forth the milk of song,
spattering like a swaying censer
out toward you in the shadow
of the faded red naves.

La cantatrice all'ascoltatrice

Grazie di avermi fatto ripensare
a quello che cantavo e dicevo.
Dopo molte prove e riprove
io non avevo ancora ben capito
che cosa avessi enunziato.
Che dal collo troncato della santa
"latte sprizzò non sangue"
mi aveva inferto un'intima paura
(temevo il latte quasi più del sangue).

Adesso, forse, un barlume
di comprendimento...
Caterina la vergine, morendo,
si è fatta al carnefice madre
(così l'alessandrina
in un sussurro parla
alla senese sanguivisionaria
da una nube di secolo all'altra).
Allora come oggi, il perdono
dev'essere risultato
a mala pena tollerabile:
come esser privati di colpo,
soffocantemente,
di quell'ossigeno d'odio
di cui si nutre la normalità
del nostro vizio diario.

The Singer to the Female Listener

I thank you for drawing my mind
to what I was singing and saying.
No matter my efforts
I still couldn't grasp
the words I'd uttered—
that from the saint's neck
"streamed milk, not blood."
They woke within me a deep dread.
(I feared milk almost more than blood).

Now, perhaps, a flicker
of comprehension…
the virgin Catherine, at her death,
made herself mother to the torturer
(so the Alexandrian girl
speaks in a whisper
to the Sienese blood-visionary
from one dark cloud
of a distant century
to another).
Such forgiveness, then as now,
must have been difficult to bear—
like being stripped, in a gasp,
of that oxygen of hate
that sustains the commonplace
of our daily vice.

Meditazione della rosa

Preferisci le rose oppure le spine?
Si chiede quando guarda le rovine
della sua a volte vita sorridendo,
come dentro se stesso discendendo.

Preferisci le spine ovvero le rose?
Forza di seduzione delle cose,
con la voce bambina del piacere…
Ma affiorano severe rose nere

subito nella mente a ricordare:
il soffio del rovaio invernale,
il tortuoso cammino nel roveto,

la traccia (sangue-cervo) sulla neve
che racconta un dolore non breve
e prepara al riposo del roseto.

Meditation on Roses

Are you one for thorns or roses,
he wonders as he gazes
at the ruins of his one-time life
and smiles, sinking into self.

Are you one for roses or thorns?
The seductive pull of things,
with their gratifying coo…
But sharp black roses bloom

in his thoughts to remind him:
the winter wind, winding
through a thicket's spiny nest,

the trail (deer blood) in the snow
that tells of grief unknown
and lays the rose bed to its rest.

Erto nel *despertar*

> "Noi per colpa nostra siamo ignobili, miserevoli e
> contrari al bene, pronti invece e volonterosi al male"
> (Francesco d'Assisi)

È bello risvegliarsi in albe vuote
con i cigli degli occhi inumiditi
prima dei diurni meccanismi e ruote
e dopo tanti sogni inariditi.

In quell'albe la pianta umana è aspersa
d'acqua di sotterranea compassione.
È, questa irrorazione, vana e persa
se autoreferente è l'emozione?

No: pietà di se stesso è il passo innanzi
dopo il primo, che è l'austerità
del disprezzo e di sé medesmo scorno.

Non vi è passo, dopo ciò, che avanzi
se non l'ultimo e terzo: carità
che consuma il "se stesso" nel suo forno.

Tall in *Despertar*

> "For by fault of our own we are rotten, miserable,
> and opposed to good, but prompt and willing to embrace evil"
> (St. Francis of Assisi)

What better than to wake to an empty dawn,
eyebrows damp, before the daily turning
of cogs and wheels, devices flicking on,
and sapped by so much desiccating dreaming.

On mornings such as these, the human plant
is dotted with beads of water, sub-terrestrial
compassions. But is all this sprinkling vain,
if the feelings are self-referential?

No—self-pity is the step that always follows
that first step one must take: a self-contempt
that scrutinizes all, a scouring self-scorn.

But after that there's no way to move forward
without charity, the third and final step,
which turns the self to ashes in its furnace.

Prossimandosi alla fiamma

Il desiderio è punta dell'osceno
e coltello appuntito d'assassino;
il desiderio è fiotto di veleno
e laccio di velluto nel giardino.

Il desiderio è scala alla purezza
ed è lacrima della trasparenza;
il desiderio vive in tenerezza,
contento della propria presenza.

Il desiderio giudica il soggetto
e viene valutato dal suo oggetto.
Desiderio non cura diletto.

Il desiderio ascolta e poco dice.
Il desiderio è come la Fenice:
la cenere d'ascesi è sua matrice.

Drawing Near the Flame

Desire is the knife point of the obscene
and the murderer's sharpened weapon,
desire is poison's gushing stream,
velvet ribbon in the garden.

Desire is the stairway to purity,
a teardrop of transparence,
desire resides in sympathy,
content with its own presence.

Desire judges the subject
and is judged by the object,
cares not for pleasurable effect.

Desire listens but hardly speaks.
Desire is like the Phoenix:
the ashes of ascesis are its matrix.

La sfida

Ha seguito le orme di Francesco
lungo un erto sentiero secco bresco:
su dai gradini della cattedrale,
nella polvere dello stradale.

Sono saliti in volta a Monteluco,
verso il romano antico bosco cupo.
Ma a un certo punto, in margine ad un fosso,
gli si rivolta come un gatto rosso:

"E tu che cosa vuoi da me, o tristo?
Le orme da seguire, son di Cristo!
Accódati al maestro e non al servo –

fatti disindividuo, fatti cervo
che non ha occhi per il santo idolo
ma segue solo il richiamo e lo stimolo".

The Challenge

He followed St. Francis's tracks,
along a steep path, parched and arid,
up cathedral stairs,
down dusty thoroughfares.

They climbed to Monteluco's peak
toward the woods—ancient, Roman, dark—
until, above a ditch, he lashed
out at him like a ginger cat:

"Why follow me, you wretch?
File behind the master, not his servant—
Christ's footprints are the trail you should be on—

de-individualize yourself, be like the fawn
who sees no sacred idol, but only goes
where he's called, and by his nose."

Epilogo

Epilogue

San Francesco d'Assisi davanti al bar "Tric-Trac"

Appena discesi a Spoleto
nel scendente crepuscolo
ancor prima di aprire le valigie
eran venuti in piazza
per ritrovare qualcosa della trascorsa estate –
forse il piccolo gatto nubiloso
che era, fantasmatico, guizzato
tra le colonne lungo il porticato
deserto del Duomo
là giù in fondo alla piazza desertata
e li aveva seguiti saltellando alla larga
giù per la Via delle Mura Ciclopiche –
ma l'anno già intercorso
aveva ritessuto un labirinto
e poi spezzato il filo:
la piazza era immutata
loro due non diversi, e proprio questo
aveva tutto cambiato.

Lui ti ha visto, Francesco, improvviso
mentre opaco fissava le lastre di pietra
di Via dell'Arringo in discesa
declivante alla piazza del Duomo.
Tutto era sghembo, anche il tavolino
sul selciato davanti al bar "Tric-Trac".
Non sapeva che dire, si annoiava
di se stesso e di lei.

St. Francis of Assisi Outside of the Cafe "Tric-Trac"

As soon as they reached Spoleto,
with twilight approaching,
before even unzipping their bags,
they went to the piazza
to find something they'd left a summer ago—
perhaps the dusty little cat
they'd seen, spectral, slipping
between the columns along the colonnaded
desert of the Duomo,
down at the far end of the deserted piazza,
pursuing them at large, in rapid leaps,
all the way down Via delle Mura Ciclopiche—
but the bygone year
had rewoven another labyrinth
and clipped the thread:
the piazza remained unchanged,
they too, unaltered—which was in fact the sign
that all had changed.

He saw you, Francis, by chance
while staring blankly at the sheets of stone
on Via dell'Arringo, that steep decline
leading down to Piazza del Duomo.
All was askew, even the table
on the cobbles outside of the Cafe "Tric-Trac."
He had nothing to say,
was bored with himself, and her.

Ma poi, d'un tratto:
ti ha veduto strisciare
come un gran verme serale –
la pallida lunetta della tonsura, i gomiti
in alto sporgenti
a puntellare le mani che arrancavano
strascinandoti lungo la discesa.
Francesco stralancato
discongiunto bistorto: ti sei preso
l'inutile peso
della loro noia.
Questa così gratuita penitenza
ha fatto finalmente vergognare
l'uomo seduto al tavolino; è pronto –
a che cosa?
Non ha avuto la forza di narrarle
ciò che stava vedendo.
Continuano a tacere
in uno sgomento silenzio
che già sta cancellando interi mesi
dall'anno che per essi si prepara.

Ma tu, Francesco, continui:
aggrampellato al suolo serpeggiando
e sopra gli scalini rimbalzando
tenti di far sentire ai due seduti
che si sono irretiti in telaragne
di dubbi e di pensieri troppo piccoli;
che oscillano nell'altalena
della dialettica frode:
desiderio, non-desiderio…

But then, there you were—
he saw you slithering
like some giant, nocturnal worm,
the pale half-moon of your tonsure, elbows
jutting far out
to leverage your hands, as you crawled
along the slope.
Contorted, double-knotted,
disjointed Francis: you gained yourself
the useless burden
of their boredom.
Such gratuitous penitence
at last ashamed the man
at the cafe table; he's ready now—
but for what?
He could find no courage to tell her
of the sight unfolding before him.
So they went on saying nothing
in the stunned silence,
already busy erasing entire months
from the year ahead.

But you, Francis, keep on moving:
hugging the earth and snaking forward,
lumbering up and over the steps,
doing all you can to make the couple see
that they're wound in a spider's web
of miniscule doubts and thoughts;
that they're wobbling on the swing
of a false dialectic:
desire, lack of desire…

Ma via, via da questi involvimenti!
Ognuno di quei due deve tentare
di visibilizzare
l'altro; e il prezzo per questo da pagare
è rendere invisibile se stesso.

Enough, enough with these entanglements!
Each of them must strain
to make the other visible:
and, of course, in compensation
become invisible themselves.

Notes

[Among Curtains]
Thomas Becket (1119/1120-1270), Archbishop of Canterbury, assassinated in that church by followers of King Henry II. The Archbishop is the hero of T.S. Eliot's *Murder in the Cathedral*. On the suggestion of Martina Della Casa, I revised the translation of the last line in the Latin text quoted here.

[Hecate]
The mythological Greek goddess reigning over the shadows and the night.

[Monteluco]
Monteluco is a hill outside Spoleto, home to a sacred wood of ancient evergreen oaks. Roman in origin, the area was subsequently occupied by Anchorites, Benedictines, and Franciscans.

[Via Vaita de Domo]
Since perhaps the second half of the fifth century CE, during Byzantine rule, and up until the seventeenth century, Spoleto was divided into ten neighborhoods called *vaite* or *guaite* (with a layout that perhaps alludes to the ideal blueprint of New Jerusalem, described in the book of the *Apocalypse*). Today, the name "Vaita de Domo" refers to a road that runs beneath the escarpment of Spoleto's cathedral, the Duomo di Spoleto. (The reference here, however, is to a family name, Domo, and any link to the Duomo itself is coincidental.)

[The Animated (After St. Francis)]
The reference is to a letter by Béla Bartók (1881-1945) quoted in an unpublished film treatment on the life of the composer.

[The Student with Splitting Shoes]
The *Ricordi politici e civili* (1512-1530) by Francesco Guicciardini, a contemporary of Machiavelli. The volume is a collection of maxims on political, social, and religious topics.

[A Cat Ballad]
The quote is from a traditional Zen anecdote of uncertain origin about the spritual master Nanquan Puyuan (sometimes transcribed as "Nansen").

[The Singer to the Female Listener]
The parallel here is between Saint Catherine of Alexandria (287-305) and Saint Catherine of Siena (1347-1380).

About the text

Thanks are due to several friends and colleagues (too many to list here), and in particular to Walter Raffaelli for his support and advice, to Todd Portnowitz for his constant creative dialogue with me, to Marc Estrin and Donna Bister for their precious collaboration in putting the book together, and to Flavia Manservigi and Guido Mattia Gallerani for their diligent help with the proofs. Aside from correcting some misprints, the present text faithfully reproduces the original Italian edition (Rimini: Raffaelli, 2013) plus some new explanatory notes.

About Fomite

A fomite is a medium capable of transmitting infectious organisms from one individual to another.

"The activity of art is based on the capacity of people to be infected by the feelings of others." Tolstoy, *What Is Art?*

Writing a review on Amazon, Good Reads, Shelfari, Library Thing or other social media sites for readers will help the progress of independent publishing. To submit a review, go to the book page on any of the sites and follow the links for reviews. Books from independent presses rely on reader to reader communications.

For more information or to order any of our books, visit
http://www.fomitepress.com/FOMITE/Our_Books.html

More Titles from Fomite...

Novels
Joshua Amses — *During This, Our Nadir*
Joshua Amses — *Raven or Crow*
Joshua Amses — *The Moment Before an Injury*
Jaysinh Birjepatel — *The Good Muslim of Jackson Heights*
Jaysinh Birjepatel — *Nothing Beside Remains*
David Brizer — *Victor Rand*
Dan Chodorkoff — *Loisaida*
David Cleveland — *Time's Betrayal*
Paula Closson Buck — *Summer on the Cold War Planet*
Roger Coleman — *Skywreck Afternoons*
Marc Estrin — *Hyde*
Marc Estrin — *Kafka's Roach*
Marc Estrin — *Speckled Vanities*
Zdravka Evtimova — *In the Town of Joy and Peace*
Zdravka Evtimova — *Sinfonia Bulgarica*
Daniel Forbes — *Derail This Train Wreck*
Greg Guma — *Dons of Time*

Richard Hawley — *The Three Lives of Jonathan Force*
Lamar Herrin — *Father Figure*
Michael Horner — *Damage Control*
Ron Jacobs — *All the Sinners Saints*
Ron Jacobs — *Short Order Frame Up*
Ron Jacobs — *The Co-conspirator's Tale*
Scott Archer Jones — *A Rising Tide of People Swept Away*
Maggie Kast — *A Free Unsullied Land*
Darrell Kastin — *Shadowboxing with Bukowski*
Coleen Kearon — *Feminist on Fire*
Coleen Kearon — *#triggerwarning*
Jan Englis Leary — *Thicker Than Blood*
Diane Lefer — *Confessions of a Carnivore*
Rob Lenihan — *Born Speaking Lies*
Colin Mitchell — *Roadman*
Ilan Mochari — *Zinsky the Obscure*
Gregory Papadoyiannis — *The Baby Jazz*
Andy Potok — *My Father's Keeper*
Kathryn Roberts — *Companion Plants*
Robert Rosenberg — *Isles of the Blind*
Fred Russell — *Rafi's World*
Ron Savage — *Voyeur in Tangier*
David Schein — *The Adoption*
Lynn Sloan — *Principles of Navigation*
L.E. Smith — *The Consequence of Gesture*
L.E. Smith — *Travers' Inferno*
L.E. Smith — *Untimely RIPped*
Bob Sommer — *A Great Fullness*
Tom Walker — *A Day in the Life*
Susan V. Weiss — *My God, What Have We Done?*
Peter M. Wheelwright — *As It Is On Earth*
Suzie Wizowaty — *The Return of Jason Green*

Poetry

Antonello Borra — *Alfabestiario*
Antonello Borra — *AlphaBetaBestiaro*

David Cavanagh — *Cycling in Plato's Cave*
James Connolly — *Picking Up the Bodies*
Greg Delanty — *Loosestrife*
Mason Drukman — *Drawing on Life*
J. C. Ellefson — *Foreign Tales of Exemplum and Woe*
Tina Escaja — *Caida Libre/Free Fall*
Anna Faktorovich — *Improvisational Arguments*
Barry Goldensohn — *Snake in the Spine, Wolf in the Heart*
Barry Goldensohn — *The Hundred Yard Dash Man*
Barry Goldensohn — *The Listener Aspires to the Condition of Music*
R. L. Green — *When You Remember Deir Yassin*
Kate Magill — *Roadworthy Creature, Roadworthy Craft*
Tony Magistrale — *Entanglements*
Andreas Nolte — *Mascha: The Poems of Mascha Kaléko*
Sherry Olson — *Four-Way Stop*
Janice Miller Potter — *Meanwell*
Joseph D. Reich — *Connecting the Dots to Shangrila*
Joseph D. Reich — *The Hole That Runs Through Utopia*
Joseph D. Reich — *The Housing Market*
Joseph D. Reich — *The Derivation of Cowboys and Indians*
Kennet Rosen and Richard Wilson — *Gomorrah*
Fred Rosnblum — *Vietnumb*
David Schein — *My Murder and Other Local News*
Harold Schweizer — *Miriam's Book*
Scott T. Starbuck — *Industrial Oz*
Scott T. Starbuck — *Hawk on Wire*
Seth Steinzor — *Among the Lost*
Seth Steinzor — *To Join the Lost*
Susan Thomas — *The Empty Notebook Interrogates Itself*
Susan Thomas — *In the Sadness Museum*
Paolo Valesio and Todd Portnowitz — *La Mezzanotte di Spoleto / Midnight in Spoleto*
Sharon Webster — *Everyone Lives Here*
Tony Whedon — *The Tres Riches Heures*
Tony Whedon — *The Falkland Quartet*
Claire Zoghb — *Dispatches from Everest*

Stories
Jay Boyer — *Flight*
Michael Cocchiarale — *Still Time*
Neil Connelly — *In the Wake of Our Vows*
Catherine Zobal Dent — *Unfinished Stories of Girls*
Zdravka Evtimova —*Carts and Other Stories*
John Michael Flynn — *Off to the Next Wherever*
Derek Furr — *Semitones*
Derek Furr — *Suite for Three Voices*
Elizabeth Genovise — *Where There Are Two or More*
Andrei Guriuanu — *Body of Work*
Zeke Jarvis — *In A Family Way*
Jan Englis Leary — *Skating on the Vertical*
Marjorie Maddox — *What She Was Saying*
William Marquess — *Boom-shacka-lacka*
Gary Miller — *Museum of the Americas*
Jennifer Anne Moses — *Visiting Hours*
Peter Nash — *Parsimony*
Martin Ott — *Interrogations*
Jack Pulaski — *Love's Labours*
Charles Rafferty — *Saturday Night at Magellan's*
Ron Savage — *What We Do For Love*
Fred Skolnik— *Americans and Other Stories*
Lynn Sloan — *This Far Is Not Far Enough*
L.E. Smith — *Views Cost Extra*
Caitlin Hamilton Summie — *To Lay To Rest Our Ghosts*
Susan Thomas — *Among Angelic Orders*
Tom Walker — *Signed Confessions*
Silas Dent Zobal — *The Inconvenience of the Wings*

Odd Birds
Micheal Breiner — *the way none of this happened*
J. C. Ellefson — *Under the Influence*
David Ross Gunn — *Cautionary Chronicles*
Andrei Guriuanu — *The Darkest City*
Gail Holst-Warhaft — *The Fall of Athens*

Roger Leboitz — *A Guide to the Western Slopes and the Outlying Area*
dug Nap— *Artsy Fartsy*
Delia Bell Robinson — *A Shirtwaist Story*
Peter Schumann — *Bread & Sentences*
Peter Schumann — *Charlotte Salomon*
Peter Schumann — *Faust 3*
Peter Schumann — *Planet Kasper, Volumes One and Two*
Peter Schumann — *We*

Plays
Stephen Goldberg — *Screwed and Other Plays*
Michele Markarian — *Unborn Children of America*

www.ingramcontent.com/pod-product-compliance
Lightning Source LLC
Chambersburg PA
CBHW021440080526
44588CB00009B/612